Horse Sense and Nonsense

A Survival Guide for Horse Lovers

By Cindy Hale
Illustrations by Jean Abernethy

A Division of BowTie, Inc.®
Irvine, California

Karla Austin, *Business Operations Manager*
Nick Clemente, *Special Consultant*
Barbara Kimmel, *Managing Editor*
Jarelle S. Stein, *Editor*
Jessica Knott, *Production Supervisor*
Cover and layout design by Amy Stirnkorb

The horses in this book are referred to as she and he in alternating chapters unless their genders are apparent from the activity discussed.

Library of Congress Cataloging-in-Publication Data

Hale, Cindy.
  Horse sense and nonsense : a survival guide for horse lovers / By Cindy Hale.
      p. cm.
  ISBN-13: 978-1-931993-94-4
  ISBN-10: 1-931993-94-7
  1. Horses. 2. Horsemanship. I. Title.

  SF285.H35 2007
  636.1—dc22
                        2006037950

BowTie Press®
A Division of BowTie, Inc.
3 Burroughs
Irvine, CA 92618

Printed and bound in Singapore
10 9 8 7 6 5 4 3 2 1

Dedication

For my horse-husband, Ron,
who has been gracious enough to keep his sense of humor

Contents

Introduction

Welcome to the World of Horses

So. You're a certified horse lover. Do you realize what you've gotten yourself into? Horses will influence every aspect of your life, from the clothes you wear to the excuses you concoct to avoid unpleasant social activities. If at times you feel a little bit overwhelmed, don't fret. Every horse lover feels that way at first. But soon, about the time you realize you can never quite get that last bit of hay dust out of your hair, you'll start to relax.

Take a deep breath, and cozy up for an entertaining, educational read. In the past, horses never came with a user's guide or an owner's manual—but they do now.

Chapter 1

Know Your Breeds

There are 114,000 breeds of horses in the world. OK, that's an exaggeration. But there are a lot, and whatever your tastes may be, at least one breed of horse will strike your fancy. Here's a brief look at a few of the more popular breeds and types of horses you'll find hanging around your local watering trough:

Breeds

Specialized breeds of horses have been created through modern matchmaking techniques. Registries monitor and maintain the hallowed bloodlines, ensuring that every purebred horse deserves to wear the family crest.

American Quarter Horse

The breed's name is derived from its fabled ability to sprint for a quarter of a mile. However, the American Quarter Horse is more respected for the inherent ability to outsmart a wily cow on the ranch. Cowboys love the American Quarter Horse. Cows . . . not so much.

Appaloosa

Once a well-kept secret of the Native Americans who lived
in the American Northwest, the versatile Appaloosa
is hard to overlook. With his polka-dotted coat
and striped hooves, he's forever in danger
of being arrested by the fashion police.

Arabian

Descended from native horses that roamed the Middle Eastern deserts, the Arabian is the purest of all horse breeds and has been used as the foundation for many other breeds of horses. This not only gives the Arabian incredible bragging rights but also accounts for those huge Arabian horse family reunions.

Paint Horse

Paint Horses resemble their American Quarter Horse and Thoroughbred relatives but with splashy, white markings. Think of the Paint as the standard model pleasure horse with a color option. (When buying a Paint Horse, inquire about the free gift with purchase: a lifetime supply of stain-removing shampoo.)

 16

Thoroughbred

For centuries, the Thoroughbred has been genetically programmed to be a racehorse. This focus on racing has made Thoroughbreds fleet and courageous.

It has also caused them to have an unwavering devotion to really short people.

Types

Can't separate spots from dots? If identifying a specific breed gives you a headache, you may wish to merely acquaint yourself with some of the generalized types of horses.

Draft Horses

The stevedores of the equine world, the various draft breeds are kind-hearted workhorses. Perpetually plus-size, draft horses must defend themselves against the taunts from svelte breeds of horses. "Really," they're forever saying, "we don't overeat. It's our metabolism."

Ponies

Ponies are not small horses; they are a separate species of equine known scientifically as *equinitas furballis*. However, savvy horse lovers the world over refer to ponies collectively by their more popular designation: the Spawn of Satan.

FEED ROOM

19

Warmbloods

Cross the euphemistically cold-blooded (patient) draft horse with the so-called hot-blooded (energetic) Thoroughbred and what do you have? An elephant-size horse with dance moves? Well, close. You have, in generic terms, a warmblood. With a compliant disposition and an impressive physical stature, this horse is supremely gifted for the disciplines of dressage and jumping. At least, that's the idea.

Chapter 2

Western Riding:
Do You Want to Be a Cowboy?

The western style of riding was developed for ranch work. Oh, the romance of the Old West! Oh, the beauty of the open range! Oh, the saddle sores from sitting on the back of a horse for eight hours! Are you sure you still want to ride like a cowboy? If your answer is yes, the following is a list of what you'll need before your inaugural "Yeehaw!"

First, you'll need a **western saddle,** which is inviting and comfortable, much like an overstuffed recliner. Alas, it also weighs about as much as your sofa, which can lead to embarrassing moments when it comes time to tack up.

All western riders need a **cowboy hat**. It will shade your eyes from the sun. Plus, it adds an extra four inches to your height.

Another necessary item is a big, shiny, **silver belt buckle**. In order to create the proper visual impact, your belt buckle must approximate the size of a vehicular license plate.

ARMOR! I LIKE IT!

You might also consider a pair of **chaps**. These leather pants zip over your jeans to protect your legs from thorns and bramble. A bonus: instant Halloween costume!

No western outfit would be complete without a pair of **boots**. Buy the fanciest, most ornate pair you can afford. Then immediately thrash and abuse them so you don't look like a dude who's just bought a fancy, ornate pair of boots.

Adorn your new boots with a pair of **spurs**. That pointed, spinning wheel on the spur is called the rowel. Even if the rowel will never touch the sides of your horse, it's vitally necessary. That's what will allow you to achieve the legendary jingle-jangle sound effect.

An indispensable western accessory is the **lariat**, which is a small rope. Unless you're adept at handling the lariat, it's best to leave it in its off-the-rack, coiled position. Otherwise, you may end up compromising the circulation in one of your extremities.

You'll be a true western rider when you've mastered **the lingo**. Practice saying, "I would've tagged that maverick dogie down by the draw, but my lariat got tangled in my buckskin's mecate."

Chapter 3

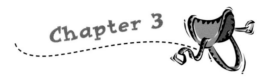

English Riding: How Good Do You Look in Tweed?

English riding evokes the high-society tradition of foxhunting. All that tallyho stuff has been ridden into obscurity, but you can still pretend you're part of the upper crust of humanity. Why, your family will hardly recognize you! But before you start genuflecting to the queen, make sure you have the gear that will make you look and sound like an English rider.

Become acquainted with the **English saddle**. Legend says that early versions were used as devices of torture. Indeed, the minimalist design of an English saddle demands incredible strength in your thighs. When you can crack a walnut between your knees, you are ready to ride.

Because it's a foregone conclusion that you're going to fall off at least once, make sure you're wearing a **safety helmet**. Abandon all illusions about coquettish coiffures; you're doomed to suffer from helmet hair.

Riding in an English saddle will be more comfortable (ha!) if you're wearing a pair of **breeches**. Made of fabric more forgiving than denim, breeches won't chafe your legs as you struggle to remain upright in the English saddle. While shopping for your first pair of the form-fitting, stretchy garment, you may worry that breeches make your butt look big. They do.

All English riders yearn for a pair of tall, snug black **boots**. They'll support your wobbly ankles and make your calves appear long and slender (a bonus). If the boots cause your toes to go numb, impair the movement of your ankles, and promote blisters at the backs of your knees, then they fit perfectly.

For fashion's sake, strap a pair of spurs to your boots. Thanks to their demure appearance, English spurs are generally more ornamental than functional. In fact, you may even forget that you are wearing a pair. However, you'll remember soon enough if you happen to make a mad dash for the tack room, hook your spurs together, and trip yourself.

Your wardrobe isn't complete without a **hunt coat**. This little bit of haute couture harkens back to the days of dressing up for a morning ride to the hounds. And what could be more appropriate for riding outdoors in the sun than a long-sleeved, tightly tailored wool blazer?

The **riding crop** is a trademark accessory of an English rider. Although meant to serve as an instrument of humankind's dominance over the horse, the crop more often comes in handy for emphatic gestures as you embellish your latest riding saga. Just be careful not to raise a welt when you absent-mindedly smack your own leg in a fit of dramatic flair.

Finally, you'll be an authentic English equestrian when you can speak **the lingo**. Feel comfortable saying, "I saw the long spot to the oxer, but my horse chipped and the martingale snapped!"

Chapter 4

A Beginner's Guide to Horse Buying

Once you're thoroughly smitten with horses, merely riding isn't enough for you. No, you've gone over the brink and decided to buy your own horse. If this is not corrected with intense counseling, then heed our advice and follow these instructions.

Honesty, Acceptance, and Poverty

First, honestly evaluate your horsemanship skills. Your skill level should be a major factor in deciding which horse to purchase. You might envision yourself galloping into the sunset aboard a spirited black stallion, but in reality, you may be better suited for plodding along on Old Pokey.

Next, accept that there are no perfect horses. Each one will have some flaw in conformation or disposition, much like the people you dated in high school. Buying a horse is like playing the dating game: you can overlook some flaws, but others will make you cringe and search for another date to the prom. For example, there are horses with front legs that seem forever fixed in ballet's first position. Unless you are a rabid supporter of all things dance, do not take this horse home.

Then there are the horses with adorable little quirks. One is the habit of spooking, in which the horse swears there is a monster lurking around every corner. This propensity makes every ride an adventure. Although you may consider yourself a thrill seeker, you're better off getting your adrenaline rush by riding something much safer. Like a roller coaster. Or a freight train.

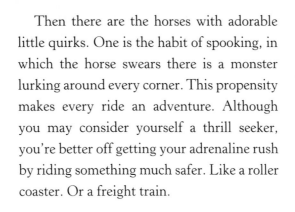

51

Finally, heed the First Law of Horse Buying: the price of your dream horse will exceed your budget by $500. This will force you to contemplate the fair market value of every item in your household. You will finally comprehend that line from Shakespeare's *King Richard III*, "My kingdom for a horse!"

Six Steps to Success

Buying a horse is like adding a new member to your family. If you tire of the horse, you can't just toss him aside. If your in-laws wear out their welcome, you wouldn't stick them on the next bus out of town, would you? *Would you?* Of course you wouldn't. To ensure that your horse enjoys the same level of permanence in your family, follow these steps before you make a life-altering purchase.

Always select a horse that is easy to handle. If the horse whirls around on the end of the lead rope like a kite in a hurricane, he is not easy to handle.

Take the prospective horse on a test ride away from his home. This will reveal his true character. Have a search party on standby in case you're not back in an hour.

When you've settled on a horse, have a veterinarian certify that the horse is healthy and sound. This is referred to as a prepurchase exam. During it, the vet will evaluate the horse's vision, listen for a strong heart and clear lungs, and flex the leg joints to check for arthritis. If you're lucky, you'll also get to pay for a full set of X-rays! This initial visit will mark the beginning of your relationship with your veterinarian. Soon you'll realize that your horse enjoys better health care than anyone in your family.

If you don't have horse property, find a local boarding stable. A suitable stable will offer your horse a roof over his head, maid service, and several meals a day. Although you may prefer to have your horse live with you, disregard the impulse to remodel a spare bedroom into a stall. Your neighbors will notice.

Upon purchasing your horse, take the customary trip to the tack store. Who knew that a horse needed so much stuff? A halter, a lead rope, a feed bucket, brushes, leg wraps, a fly spray, a hoof pick, a coat polish, shampoo, a mane comb, hoof dressing, tail detangling gel . . . with a list so overwhelming, it's best to just buy one of everything. Two if they're a pretty color.

Finally, spend hours contemplating a name for your horse. Choose one that's pleasing to the equine ear. However, try not to feel hurt when Sir Fluffy responds more eagerly to the sound of grain being poured into his feed bucket.

Chapter 5

Riding Lessons: What Fun!

Horseback riding is best practiced only after you have received some competent instruction. Before signing up for riding lessons, observe the instructor at work to make sure he or she has a teaching style that suits your personality.

Some riding instructors are like friendly mentors, and their stables exude the atmosphere of a day spa. Why, you can even smell the fragrance of patchouli potpourri in the tack room!

Other riding instructors are like drill sergeants, and they run their stables like an army barracks. Who knew horses could be trained to salute?

You'll learn many skills from riding lessons. For example, you'll be taught how to bridle a horse that thinks she's a giraffe.

You'll also learn how to sit properly in a saddle. Believe it or not, you shouldn't bounce around like a marionette at the trot.

No doubt you'll take your lessons on a school horse. These four-legged babysitters have seen your kind many times before. To maintain their dignity (and destroy yours), they've acquired some clever habits, such as coming to abrupt stops midstride to (allegedly) scratch their faces. As you progress, you may be taught advanced skills such as jumping. This is where you trust your horse to carry you through the air over an obstacle constructed of heavy wooden poles and planks. Hey, you only live once!

At what point during riding lessons will you know when you've achieved some mastery of horsemanship? You'll be able to tack up a horse on your own without the risk of personal injury, and fellow equestrians will no longer perceive you as a potential threat to their safety.

Chapter 6

The Mechanics of Forward Motion

One of the primary goals of riding lessons is learning how to effectively and safely shift your horse from one gear to the next. Much like an automobile, a horse comes equipped with several gears: forward, neutral, reverse, fast, and faster. A prudent rider will fully understand how to operate a horse before climbing aboard.

You must acquaint yourself with the bridle. The bridle, which goes on the horse's head while the horse holds the bit in his mouth, is undeniably the most important piece of tack because it's your horse's braking system. Yes, that's right: A 1,000-pound beast is controlled by a few flimsy straps of leather and 8 ounces of stainless steel.

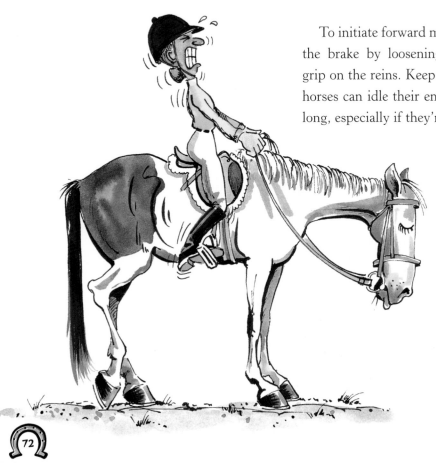

To initiate forward motion, you must release the brake by loosening your white-knuckled grip on the reins. Keep in mind, however, that horses can idle their engines in neutral all day long, especially if they're standing in the shade of a tree. Squeeze the horse's sides with your legs. If you squeeze so hard that your face is the color of a plum, yet you remain at a standstill, you may have to resort to other tactics.

Try nudging the horse with a bump of your heels. Never kick the horse with your heels, as this could produce an undesirable effect. Consult the following equations for clarification.

HEELS + BUMP = YOU ARE TROTTING

HEELS + KICK = YOU ARE BUCKED OFF

Some horses respond to verbal cues such as "Giddy-up." Others respect commands such as "Trot!" Then there are horses that prefer polite requests such as a kissing sound or a cluck-cluck. However, avoid outright pleading as that will only make you appear weak and needy to the horse.

Once your horse is moving forward, steer him with the reins. Have in mind a specific destination, and make a commitment to ride toward it. This is very important because the horse has only two destinations in his mind: freedom and the barn.

74

If you are an experienced rider with a need for speed, you can urge your horse into a gallop. Lean slightly forward in the saddle (so that the wind will really blow through your hair), and hug your horse's sides with your legs until he attains the desired RPMs. How exhilarating! If you begin to outpace the cars on the turnpike, you might want to slow down.

To stop your horse's forward motion, simply pull back on the reins and say "Whoa." Some horses are prone to stopping abruptly. This will allow you to experience firsthand one of the immutable laws of physics—inertia.

Chapter 7

Let's Go for a Trail Ride!

After achieving your goals in riding lessons, why not test them out on your own? A trail ride is the perfect way to start.

A trail ride is meant to be a leisurely excursion in which you commune with Mother Nature. Statistics show, however, that 50 percent of all trail rides include some element of calamity. To improve your odds of coming back intact, choose a trail that is well marked and free of predators, such as cougars and dirt bikers.

Once you select a site for your trail ride, invite your best barn buddy for company. The two of you must pack your gear. This means that you bring along everything you own that has anything to do with a horse. Just be sure that in addition to your fleece saddle seat cover, your ergonomic riding breeches, and your custom saddle bags filled with takeout from the gourmet deli, you also take along water, insect repellent, and a map.

Next, convince your horses that they, too, want to go for a trail ride. Offering them a look at travel brochures may motivate them to get into the trailer.

Upon your arrival at the trailhead, unload your horses. Beware! Your horses might consider making a run for it. That's how the mustangs got started.

83

Preparation is the key to a successful trail ride. You can introduce your horses to some of the natural elements they'll discover on the trail in the safety of their own stable. For example, if you haven't acquainted your horses with free-flowing water ahead of time, you may discover they have no intention of crossing a stream. But the view of the other side is nice, isn't it? To prevent sudden outbreaks of hydrophobia on the trail, work at home, teaching your horses to step into and through puddles of water. Do not allow them to beg for galoshes.

When you do get back to the trailhead, allow yourself to savor the moment. Oh, if only there were merit badges for surviving one's first trail ride! Try not to feel disheartened, however, when the horses shove each other out of the way as they scurry into the trailer to head home. Being herd animals, horses are not the best tourists in the animal kingdom.

You'll come home with plenty of souvenirs to commemorate your first trail ride. These will include burrs, thorns, sunburn, poison ivy, minor abrasions, and the occasional wood tick. And yet you'll be planning your next trail ride by nightfall.

Chapter 8

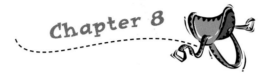

Beware the Bored Horse

Horses are very industrious animals, and if they aren't kept busy, they'll find ways to keep themselves entertained. They're very resourceful at creating hobbies; here are just a few of them.

Remodeling the barn: To a horse, every stable is a fixer-upper. Unfortunately, this compulsion to redesign the homestead can reduce any wooden structure to a mere pile of splinters overnight.

Scuba diving: Although horses have a rough time getting swim fins over their hooves, they love to go for a dip on a summer afternoon, especially when the whole herd stops by. Nothing spells fun like tipping over the water trough to create an instant wading pool!

Magic acts: Who doesn't enjoy the legerdemain skills of an amateur magician? One of the first tricks a horse learns is how to make his shoes disappear. Remember that quartet of $120 shoes your farrier just nailed on? Abracadabra! Now there are only three.

Horticulture: It is only fitting that the world's consummate grazer would refine his grass-cutting talents to become a gardener extraordinaire. Turn a horse loose near a flower bed, and you'll soon have a topiary garden you never imagined.

Fashion design: Horses born with a creative streak often channel their energy into retrofitting their clothing. Be prepared to amass a collection of horse blankets with missing buckles, bridles with broken reins, and saddles grooved with teeth marks.

Gymnastics: Practice makes perfect, and many a horse aims to score that perfect 10 for Equine Olympic feats such as bucking, rearing, and of course, leaping to the side just as the rider tries to hop into the saddle.

How can you keep your horse occupied so that he doesn't indulge in devious leisure-time activities? You can try getting some toys for his stall. Or buy him a television.

Chapter 9

The Gentle Art of Horsekeeping

Maintaining a clean, safe, pleasant environment is important for your horse's physical and mental well-being. You may end up exhausted, frazzled, and broke, but your horse will be content. And isn't that what's important? Here are a few tips on how to keep your horse happy and healthy.

Get a good muck cart: The muck cart is a heavy-duty, glorified wheelbarrow. As an integral part of daily stall cleaning chores, it will become your new best friend. Feel free to give it a name. You may not own a fancy schmancy car, but by golly, you can sure push around a spectacular muck cart!

Find a good fork: What goes along with a fine muck cart? A state-of-the-art muck fork! The best kind doubles as a rake and a pooper scooper, so you can multitask in the manure department. Your kitchen may be in violation of local health and safety codes, but your horse's stall will be immaculate!

Don't buy baloney: When selecting feed for your horse, remember that most horses will turn up their discerning noses at anything less than A1 quality feed. Don't even bother with hay that smells musty or feels brittle and dry. Your horse will simply make a grand display of his disgust by tossing it over the barn door, like so much pasty pasta. To put it in human terms, why should your horse eat macaroni when a short-term hunger strike will get him capellini pomodoro?

Pad the pantry: Horses like to have an abundance of snack foods around the barn just in case company stops by. Stock the equine pantry with goodies such as sugar cubes, carrots, peppermints, horse biscuits, watermelon, red licorice, pretzels, molasses, and apples. The beverage of choice is lukewarm orange soda pop (nondiet, of course).

Ready the stockade: The most thankless task of horsekeeping is waging the battle against flies. Compile an arsenal of various sprays, wipes, kill jars, and sticky strips. Learn more about flies than most entomology students. Then sit back and watch the swarms come, nonetheless.

Don't forget the music: Finally, to provide a soothing ambience to the stable, consider playing music during the daytime. Select a radio station that caters to country-western or smooth jazz. Avoid heavy metal. When horses begin playing air guitar, pretty much anything can happen.

103

Chapter 10

You Know You're a Horse Lover When . . .

My, how your life has changed since the first time you groomed a horse! You no longer care when horse hair clings to your wool sweater or sticks to your front teeth. Here are some other ways to tell that you're now a bona fide horse lover.

You see nothing odd about naming your son Blaze or your daughter Flicka. Fortunately, you draw the line at Secretariat; because it has so many letters, it'll never fit on a kindergartner's name tag.

You've become known for your personal scent: *Eau de Barn Muck.*

From home repair to craft projects, you've discovered 101 uses for baling twine.

An amazing transference of toiletries has taken place. First you shampooed your horse's mane and tail with your salon hair products. Then your horse's hoof emollient became your favorite hand cream.

The grocery clerks recognize you as the only customer who buys that ten-pound sack of industrial-size gnarled carrots.

To reach the milk and butter in your refrigerator, you first have to push past a bottle of horse antibiotics and a tube of dewormer.

Rather than toss out old tack, you incorporate it into your home decor.

At family potlucks, your relatives are often suspicious of any food you prepare. You scoff when they happen to find a hair in your homemade casserole. "Oh, it's sorrel colored," you say with a shrug. "Relax. It's just from Ol' Sparky."

Your dress shoes are your one pair of loafers without arena dirt plastered on the sole. This makes you quite the trendsetter at formal affairs.

As a horse lover, you're greeted with whinnies, nuzzled by a soft nose, and carried over the earth with the wind in your face. Let the rest of the world laugh at you. You're the luckiest person alive!

About the Author

Cindy Hale is a lifelong horsewoman. She has competed at all levels of horse shows in western, saddleseat, and driving events and is a thirty-year hunter and jumper veteran. A former schoolteacher, Cindy has turned her love of all things horse into a second career as a regular feature writer with *Horse Illustrated* magazine, for which she won a Pegasus Award in 2005 from the United States Equestrian Federation. She is the author of *Riding for the Blue* and *A Passion for Horses*. She has also contributed her experience and knowledge to *Horses USA, California Thoroughbred, The Los Angeles Times*, and various equestrian Web sites. Cindy lives in Southern California with her husband, Ron, and a pair of palomino mares.